MCR
22.95

MCR

DEC 1 4 2007

EVANSTON PUBLIC LIBRARY

3 1192 01380 2374

T5-AOK-387

xBiog Ivyquee Eting.K
Etingoff, Kim.
Ivy Queen /

HIP-HOP

Alicia Keys
Ashanti
Beyoncé
Black Eyed Peas
Busta Rhymes
Chris Brown
Christina Aguilera
Ciara
Cypress Hill
Daddy Yankee
DMX
Don Omar
Dr. Dre
Eminem
Fat Joe
50 Cent
The Game
Hip-Hop: A Short History
Hip-Hop Around the World
Ice Cube
Ivy Queen
Jay-Z
Jennifer Lopez
Juelz Santana
Kanye West

Lil Wayne
LL Cool J
Lloyd Banks
Ludacris
Mariah Carey
Mary J. Blige
Missy Elliot
Nas
Nelly
Notorious B.I.G.
OutKast
Pharrell Williams
Pitbull
Queen Latifah
Reverend Run (of Run DMC)
Sean "Diddy" Combs
Snoop Dogg
T.I.
Tupac
Usher
Will Smith
Wu-Tang Clan
Xzibit
Young Jeezy
Yung Joc

Ivy Queen is a rarity in the hip-hop world: a woman who has achieved fame. She is one of the most-recognized reggaeton stars in the world.

HipHop

Ivy Queen

Kim Etingoff

EVANSTON PUBLIC LIBRARY
CHILDREN'S DEPARTMENT
1703 ORRINGTON AVENUE
EVANSTON, ILLINOIS 60201

Mason Crest Publishers

Ivy Queen

Copyright © 2008 by Mason Crest Publishers. All rights reserved. No part of this publication may be reproduced or transmitted in any form or by any means, electronic or mechanical, including photocopying, recording, taping, or any information storage and retrieval system, without permission from the publisher.

Produced by Harding House Publishing Service, Inc.
201 Harding Avenue, Vestal, NY 13850.

MASON CREST PUBLISHERS INC.
370 Reed Road
Broomall, Pennsylvania 19008
(866)MCP-BOOK (toll free)
www.masoncrest.com

Printed in the United States of America

First Printing

9 8 7 6 5 4 3 2 1

Library of Congress Cataloging-in-Publication Data

Etingoff, Kim.
  Ivy Queen / Kim Etingoff.
    p. cm. — (Hip-hop)
  Includes bibliographical references and index.
  ISBN 978-1-4222-0295-1
  ISBN: 978-1-4222-0077-3 (series)
 1. Ivy Queen, 1972—Juvenile literature. 2. Rap musicians—Puerto Rico—Biography—Juvenile literature. I. Title.
  ML3930.I98E85 2008
  782.421649092—dc22
    [B]
                                            2007028137

Publisher's notes:
- All quotations in this book come from original sources and contain the spelling and grammatical inconsistencies of the original text.

- The Web sites mentioned in this book were active at the time of publication. The publisher is not responsible for Web sites that have changed their addresses or discontinued operation since the date of publication. The publisher will review and update the Web site addresses each time the book is reprinted.

DISCLAIMER: The following story has been thoroughly researched, and to the best of our knowledge, represents a true story. While every possible effort has been made to ensure accuracy, the publisher will not assume liability for damages caused by inaccuracies in the data, and makes no warranty on the accuracy of the information contained herein. This story has not been authorized nor endorsed by Ivy Queen.

Contents

Hip-Hop Time Line	6
1 Spotlight on the Latin Grammys	9
2 The Music	15
3 From There to Here	29
4 The Future of Ivy Queen and Reggaeton	43
Chronology	56
Accomplishments and Awards	57
Further Reading/Internet Resources	58
Glossary	60
Index	62
About the Author	64
Picture Credits	64

Hip-Hop Time Line

1970s DJ Kool Herc pioneers the use of breaks, isolations, and repeats using two turntables.

1970s Grafitti artist Vic begins tagging on New York subways.

1976 Grandmaster Flash and the Furious Five emerge as one of the first battlers and freestylers.

1982 Afrika Bambaataa tours Europe in another hip-hop first.

1980 Rapper Kurtis Blow sells a million records and makes the first nationwide TV appearance for a hip-hop artist.

1984 The track "Roxanne Roxanne" sparks the first diss war.

1988 Hip-hop record sales reach 100 million annually.

1985 The film *Krush Groove*, about the rise of Def Jam Records, is released.

1970   1980

1970s The central elements of the hip-hop culture begin to emerge in the Bronx, New York City.

1979 "Rapper's Delight," by The Sugarhill Gang, goes gold.

1974 Afrika Bambaataa organizes the Universal Zulu Nation.

1981 Grandmaster Flash and the Furious Five release *Adventures on the Wheels of Steel*.

1983 Ice-T releases his first singles, marking the earliest examples of gangsta rap.

1984 *Graffitti Rock*, the first hip-hop television program, premieres.

1986 Run DMC cover Aerosmith's "Walk this Way" and appear on the cover of *Rolling Stone*.

1988 MTV premieres *Yo! MTV Raps*.

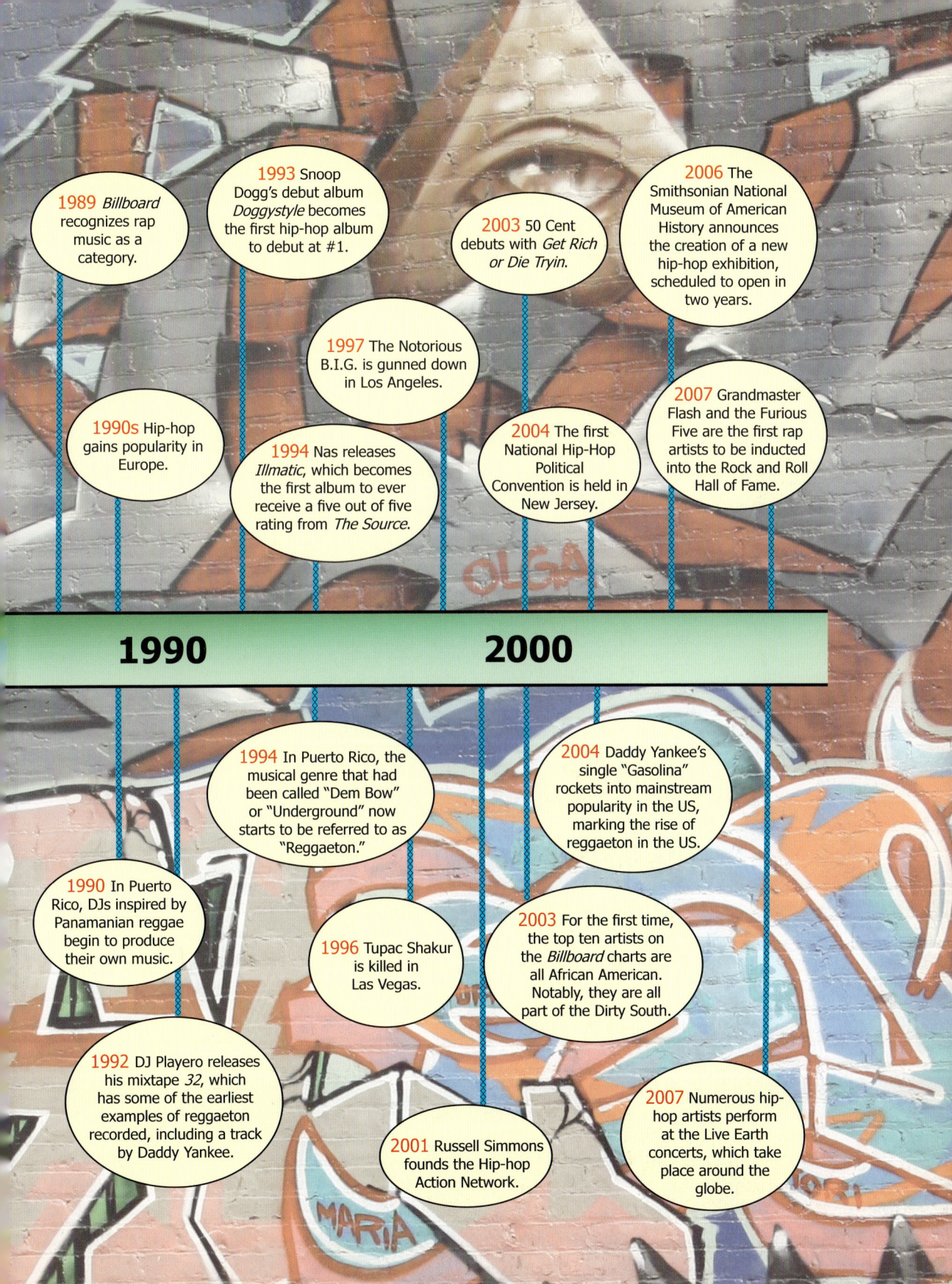

At one time, Ivy Queen was known as much for her very long fingernails as she was for her music. That has changed now: Ivy is making a name for herself all over the world as an ambassador of reggaeton music.

Spotlight on the Latin Grammys

The Latin Grammy Awards are a source of big excitement for artists of all sorts of Latin music, as well as for their fans. The Seventh Annual Latin Grammy Awards were no different; there was a buzz of discussion and articles surrounding the November 3, 2006, award date. That year the awards were held in New York City for the first time, at the famous Madison Square Garden. It was also the first time tickets were sold to the general public. Now fans could attend the awards, rock to the performances, and cheer on their favorites.

But those weren't the only firsts for the awards show. The huge awards show also received attention because it would now recognize a new *genre* of Latin music: reggaeton. That style had made an impact on the music world for a long time, but it had never received the award recognition the 2006 Latin Grammys would give it.

Ivy Queen is the best-known female making a name for herself in the reggaeton world. Okay, she's actually one of the few females who have achieved success in reggaeton. Like many forms of hip-hop, males dominate the genre. But Ivy's strong, confident voice and her wild sense of style make her stand out in her genre. That night at the Latin Grammys, she stood out as well!

Ivy Queen Makes an Appearance

One of the highlights of the Seventh Annual Latin Grammys was the *medley* of reggaeton songs performed by several of the world's biggest reggaeton stars. Wisin y Yandel and Hector "El Father" performed, and of course, so did Ivy Queen. Her number included special effects like fireworks and smoke. A group of dancers moved in the background, all adding to the excitement of the songs.

Though she hasn't won any Latin Grammys—yet—Ivy Queen has a host of other awards to her name. She can lay claim to the fact that she is one of the most-recognized reggaeton stars in the world, and not just because she is one of the few women. Being asked to perform at the Grammys says that when people think of reggaeton, they think of Ivy Queen.

Latin Music Comes to America

Choosing New York City to host the Latin Grammys meant more than just picking a convenient location for artists from the United States, Spain, and Latin America to meet. It was also recognition that Latin music was becoming an important part of U.S. *culture*, and that the people of New York City recognized the Latino influence on their city. In fact, many

SPOTLIGHT ON THE LATIN GRAMMYS

11

In 2006, the Latin Grammy Awards were held in New York City for the very first time. This signaled the growing popularity of Latin music, and of Latin stars. This poster was designed to commemorate the event.

reggaeton artists call New York City home, including Ivy Queen, who also grew up there.

Before 2006, the Latin Grammys were held in Los Angeles and Miami, both cities with large Latino populations. New York City is also home to millions of Latinos, so it makes sense for the awards show to be held in a city with such a big Latino influence. When Mayor Michael Bloomberg, who spoke in both Spanish and English, made the announcement that the awards would be hosted in New York, he said, "New

Many hip-hop stars were born or have lived in New York City, and the Big Apple is also home to many reggaeton stars, including Ivy Queen. The city's large Latino population played an important role in the birth of hip-hop, which in turn played a role in the development of reggaeton. The circle of musical influence goes on and on.

York City is the proud home to the most diverse Hispanic population in the world."

Music from Latin America is making a big impact on the rest of North America as well. Over 11.3 million people watched the Seventh Annual Latin Grammys, which was broadcast entirely in Spanish. This means that millions of Latinos in the United States and Canada were turning to Latin music, both to connect with their roots and to simply have fun.

Why Reggaeton?

Music from Latin countries, from the flamenco of Spain to Brazilian folk songs, has been around for a long time. All music evolves, changing over time to create new types that appeal to different people. In Puerto Rico, for example, a mix of many different styles has combined to form what is now called reggaeton. Even though it has only been around for a couple of decades, it is very popular in Latin American countries, especially in Puerto Rico and the Caribbean region. The organizers of the Latin Grammys realized the force that reggaeton had become, and decided to include it in 2006's award show. The 11.3 million people who tuned in to the Latin Grammys watched as Ivy Queen and other stars performed reggaeton music. They were also treated to performances of more traditional types of music such as *salsa* and *norteño*.

Reggaeton might be one of the newest expressions of Latino music—but its roots stretch far back in history.

Many young people in Puerto Rico are loyal followers of reggaeton and its artists, like Ivy Queen. Reggaeton is also popular in other Caribbean nations.

2
The Music

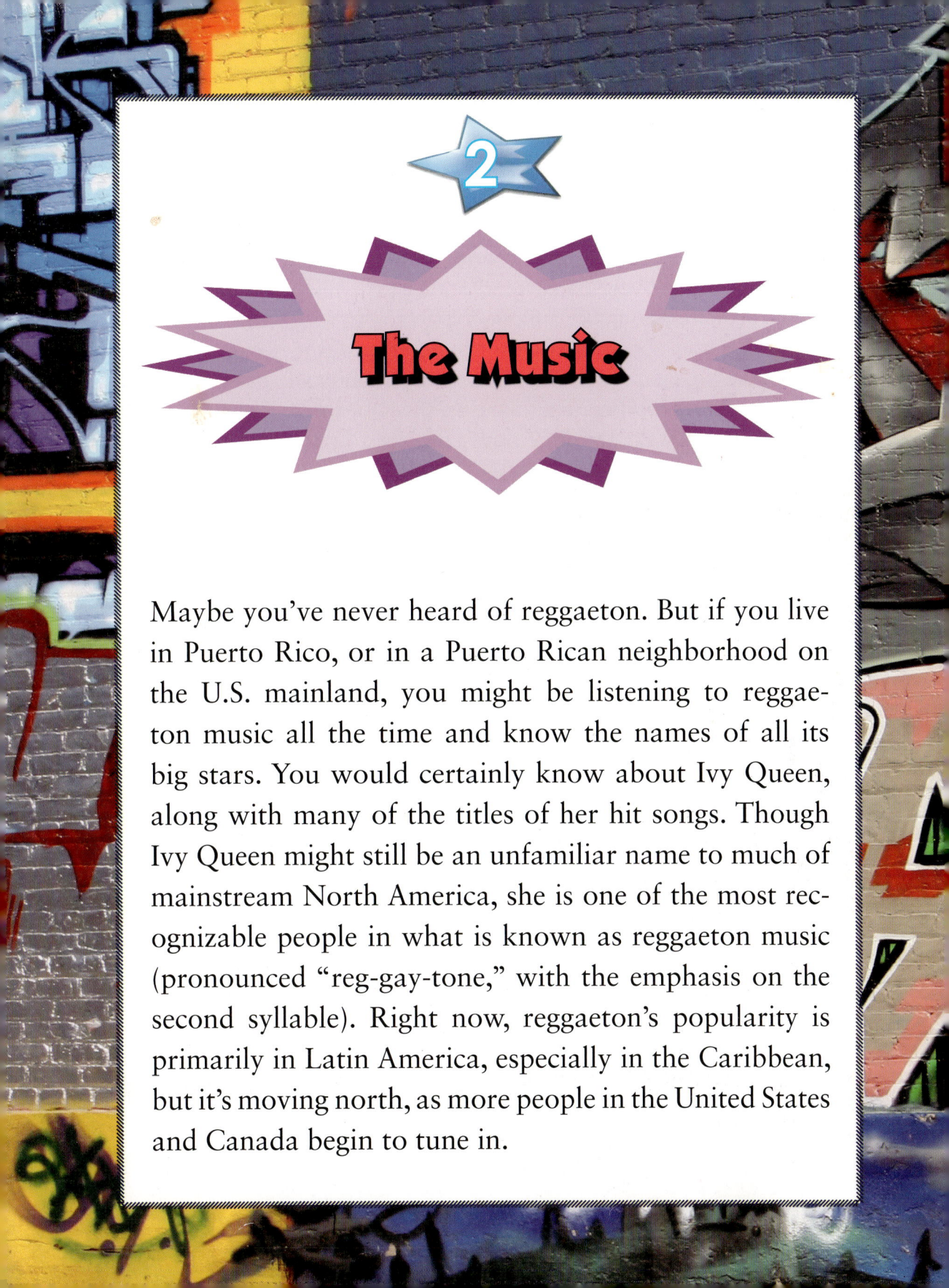

Maybe you've never heard of reggaeton. But if you live in Puerto Rico, or in a Puerto Rican neighborhood on the U.S. mainland, you might be listening to reggaeton music all the time and know the names of all its big stars. You would certainly know about Ivy Queen, along with many of the titles of her hit songs. Though Ivy Queen might still be an unfamiliar name to much of mainstream North America, she is one of the most recognizable people in what is known as reggaeton music (pronounced "reg-gay-tone," with the emphasis on the second syllable). Right now, reggaeton's popularity is primarily in Latin America, especially in the Caribbean, but it's moving north, as more people in the United States and Canada begin to tune in.

Reggaeton is a mixture of several types of music, including rap, techno, and **reggae**. Artists have combined into a distinctive, beat-heavy style popular with young people in the Caribbean region, although it has recently begun to spread well beyond that part of the world. Ivy Queen, whose name sounds like "Ee-vee," is currently one of the few women who have been able to make a name for herself in reggaeton, making her stand out in a crowd of male artists. But her uniqueness as a woman is certainly not the only thing she has to her credit; she earns her nickname as the Queen of Reggaeton because of her skill and the powerful lyrics in her songs.

What Exactly Is Reggaeton?

Reggaeton is a fairly new type of music, and the name reggaeton is even newer. Before the mid-1990s, the style was referred to as Spanish reggae, which falsely advertised it as reggae that happened to be in Spanish. The newer name, reggaeton, identifies it as something new and different.

People also sometimes confuse reggaeton with Spanish hip-hop, but while hip-hop did partly inspire reggaeton, it is not the same genre of music. Like hip-hop, reggaeton is often rapped rather than sung and it relies on drumbeats and rhythm. Its popularity with urban youth also ties together the two styles, confusing people who don't regularly listen to either kind of music. Despite its similarities to hip-hop, however, reggaeton is a truly unique style. It began in Puerto Rico in the 1980s, growing in popularity on the island during the next two decades. It draws its name from Jamaican reggae, but also grew out of American rap as well as other types of music. Reggaeton's Puerto Rican roots meant that salsa and other folk music from the Caribbean had a strong influence on the development of the genre.

Reggaeton's most distinguishing feature is its beat, called "dem bow," a name that comes from the song "Dem Bow," by Jamaican **dancehall** artist Shabba Ranks. Many reggae-

THE MUSIC

ton songs still use the same heavy beat inspired by the song, although artists also use variations on the beat. Computers, electronic keyboards, and drum machines create the characteristic sounds of reggaeton, setting it apart from more traditional music and giving it a fresh, new sound.

Now, with artists like Ivy Queen gaining fame across Latin America and in the United States, Canada, and Spain—along with artists such as Daddy Yankee, Don Omar, and Tego Calderón—reggaeton may soon be popular around the world.

If you had to pick one thing that characterizes reggaeton, it would have to be the beat. In reggaeton, it is called "dem bow." The beat was influenced by Jamaican dancehall music.

IVY QUEEN

The first artist to bring reggaeton to the attention of the world was Daddy Yankee. After beginning in small clubs in Puerto Rico, he has gone on to fill stadiums and other large venues all over the world.

It is already very popular in areas of the United States with large Puerto Rican populations, especially in big cities like Miami and New York City. Places like Madison Square Garden in New York City have recently held large, successful reggaeton concerts attended by both Latinos and people of other **ethnicities**. American music television networks, notably MTV, have also begun to cover reggaeton artists, including Ivy Queen.

New technology is one of the main reasons reggaeton music has spread from Puerto Rico so quickly. It isn't hard to find songs and artist information on YouTube, iTunes, and other Internet Web sites, allowing people all over the world almost immediate access to the genre. Older technology also plays a part in the growing interest in reggaeton: radio stations around the Americas are playing reggaeton. Several entire stations are devoted to it, while others schedule an hour or two a day to play a reggaeton program.

More Than Music

Reggaeton is much more than a style of music. The role it plays in Latino society is much like that of rap in the black community. Starting during the 1970s and 1980s in the United States, African American young people in cities began to use rap to talk about their anger at society; they rapped about poverty and racism, injustice, and hopelessness. Now, Latino youth have turned to reggaeton for the same reason. Reggaeton, like rap, lets urban Latino youth talk about their frustration at the lack of change in places like Puerto Rico, where they feel held back by older generations and traditional ways. Some songs discuss important social problems facing modern Latinos, such as immigration, racism, and unemployment.

Great Kilo, a reggaeton artist, said of his music, "Singing about problems takes the urge out of wanting to go out and burn something down." Music provides a way for young Latinos to call for change in a nonviolent, "but real," way.

Instead of trying to force change on their communities through crime and violence, reggaeton and its messages allow young people to peacefully express themselves and fight for what they believe. Victor Lopez, part of a two-man group from California called Crooked Stilo, summarizes reggaeton by saying, "It's something new, it's hot in the clubs, and people like dancing to it. Plus, the words and melodies have something to them." Reggaeton's catchy rhythm and danceable beat attract a big audience, but once a listener pays attention to the lyrics, she understands there is more to reggaeton than just good music.

The Controversy at Home

Despite the recent popularity of reggaeton, change never comes easily. The changes the younger generation are calling for, and the way in which they are demanding it, have sparked controversy in Puerto Rico. Older generations frown on reggaeton, partly because of its sometimes-crude lyrics about sex and the sexually suggestive dancing, called *perreo*, that goes with the music. Some places have even gone so far as to ban reggaeton, which makes it even more popular with young people who want to fight against authority and have fun singing and dancing. Younger people who listen to reggaeton instead of the traditionally popular salsa see their music as a way to rebel against the unchanging ways of their parents and grandparents. By singing about sex and other social issues, they hope to begin positive change, moving away from social and sexual **oppression**.

Some people are opposed to reggaeton because, like hip-hop, the lyrics are often disrespectful to women. Songs sometimes paint a picture of women as objects for men to use, and almost all songs are sung from a man's point of view. However, Ivy Queen has been able to lend the female voice to reggaeton music and fight this disrespect with her songs about

THE MUSIC

What is it about reggaeton that makes it so popular? The danceability, of course. You can't help but get caught up in the beat of the music, and once you're on the dance floor, there's no stopping you.

IVY QUEEN

Hip-hop and reggaeton are related and have many things in common. Hip-hop was born in the Bronx, where life was hard and many of the people were poor and lived in housing projects like these. In Puerto Rico, reggaeton first flourished among that nation's poor as well.

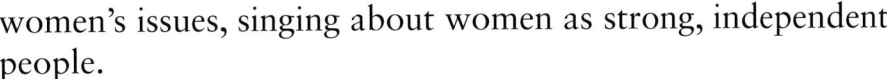

women's issues, singing about women as strong, independent people.

The way the songs treat women is just one of many things that tie reggaeton to hip-hop. Although the two kinds of music are not the same, they share many other similarities.

Hip-Hop

Though the terms are often used interchangeably, hip-hop describes a culture; rap refers to the music. Anything from graffiti, to street clothes, to a certain way of talking is considered hip-hop culture, with rap music central to the identity of this culture.

Although its Spanish cousin reggaeton is not considered to be the same as rap, the two have important connections. In many ways, reggaeton mirrors rap in its style, purpose, and history. Even its rhythms are somewhat similar. Both types of music rely on heavy beats and are meant to bring the audience to the dance floor. Both types are urban music that attract young people who want to express themselves while having fun. Parallels between reggaeton and hip-hop pop up everywhere, so a close look at where hip-hop has come from and where it's headed provides a perspective on how reggaeton has developed and what its future may be.

The development of hip-hop is very similar to reggaeton's, although in a different area of the world. It is officially said to have begun in a Bronx apartment building in the 1970s. There, DJ Kool Herc provided music for parties during the early 1970s, inspiring other artists. Kool Herc immigrated to New York City from Jamaica, and grew up listening to the sounds of reggae; like reggaeton, hip-hop owes some of its sound to the reggae of Jamaica.

Hip-hop spread quickly because of its catchy beat and meaningful lyrics, much like reggaeton did. Young urban blacks, angry at the poverty and racism they saw all around them, flocked to hip-hop. Some of the first hip-hop songs, such as "The Message" performed by Grandmaster Flash and the Furious Five, had lyrics about living in ghettos, where poverty, dirt, and crime were everywhere. All around the country, young black and Hispanic people identified with these issues. A decade or so later, Latino audiences would respond to reggaeton in the same way, using music as a way to speak out for themselves and their problems.

Hip-Hop's Expanding Audience

Today, hip-hop is regularly on top-40 charts, and the culture surrounding hip-hop is a normal sight on TV, on computers, and on the streets. Even those who might not normally listen to hip-hop's pounding beat are familiar with its rhythms from television commercials and movie soundtracks. Hip-hop's move into the **mainstream** may predict what will happen to reggaeton in the future. Already American audiences of all ethnicities are catching on to reggaeton, although it is still currently most popular with Latino young people.

During the 1990s and 2000s, hip-hop spread beyond the United States. People in other countries began to listen to it and then to adapt it to create new styles of music. Some countries, notably France, the United Kingdom, many Spanish-speaking countries, and several African countries, have thriving hip-hop cultures. Some artists, like MC Solaar from France, are famous around the world.

When hip-hop reached Puerto Rico, it mixed with other types of music to create reggaeton. Reggaeton, in its turn, is now doing the same, spreading out around the world. In the global world where we are all linked so quickly and easily through the Internet, music spreads like wildfire.

Conflict

The likeness between hip-hop and reggaeton doesn't end with their similar histories and global spread. The debate surrounding hip-hop also seems a lot like the arguments over reggaeton. Both hip-hop and reggaeton lyrics can be crude and violent, for example, alarming some people who feel these music genres lead to violence and hatred in young listeners. On one hand, crime and violence are parts of the poor, urban culture that inspires both reggaeton and hip-hop, so artists sing about those issues; those who defend these music forms say that critics are unwilling to face the reality of urban life, but that hip-hip and reggaeton speak with integrity for the streets' harsh truths. On the other hand, critics argue, many

Hip-hop and reggaeton share another characteristic. Both have been criticized for glorifying bad behavior in their songs. Sometimes the bad behavior isn't restricted to the lyrics. Several hip-hop and reggaeton musicians have spent some time behind bars.

IVY QUEEN

Today, the music that began in the streets, parks, and clubs has become mainstream. People can easily find reggaeton and hip-hop tunes and download them to their mp3 players.

songs, especially more modern ones, go well beyond merely portraying reality. Singers use swear words and **graphically** describe violent actions; they sensationalize and normalize ugliness and violence.

In the end, hip-hop pits urban youth, in many cases minorities, against middle-class society. Hip-hop's anger and frustration came from African American and Hispanic culture, inspired by poverty and racism, but its messages have attracted young people of all colors. Reggaeton, on the other hand, fights against a slightly different set of issues. Poverty is still a central theme, but so is a desire to break out of the traditional ways of Latin American countries like Puerto Rico.

The important connection is that both hip-hop and reggaeton artists recognize that music energizes youth; it's a positive channel for rage and frustration. Performers like Ivy Queen turn their own experiences into music and rhythm, allowing millions of young people to identify with their strong lyrics.

Ivy Queen has come a long way in her life and career. Through hard work—and incredible talent—Ivy Queen has become a glamorous and successful star with millions of fans.

3

From There to Here

Artists are the people who make music real, who connect the audience to the beat. In reggaeton, one woman is an expert at this. Ivy Queen has worked hard to get where she is today; she is now one of the most well-known reggaeton artists in the world.

Ivy Queen's Place in Reggaeton

Ivy Queen has been involved with reggaeton for almost the entire lifetime of the young music movement. As the only major female reggaeton artist, she has the power to communicate messages that relate uniquely to women. She takes that responsibility very seriously. In many of her songs, she sings about domestic violence, single mothers, and powerful women, subjects male artists don't usually cover. Ivy provides the female perspective on male-female issues, using her own strong image to urge other women to also be strong. Her song "Tuya Soy" ("I Am Yours") is about a wife with an unfaithful husband, and it speaks directly to Ivy's female audience.

Ivy's deep, low voice is her trademark. Its uniqueness was why many of her original fans were drawn to her. Critics were intrigued about the woman who had a voice unlike any they had ever heard. Describing it, Ivy told reporter Ramiro Burr, "God blessed me with a powerful voice. It is not feminine and not masculine. It is just a thick voice." Ivy is called *La Caballota*, "big female horse," perhaps because of her voice.

Her songs are important because of their messages. Unlike many other reggaeton artists, she does not use crude language to convey her feelings, but instead, she focuses on what she wants to say about life. Talking about her album *Sentimiento* (Emotion), she said, "Because people see us as reggaeton . . . they think one doesn't have feelings and maybe can't write the way I wrote this album." While her rhythms make people want to dance, her lyrics make her music more than just a beat, a fact she takes pride in.

The title of her second album, *The Original Rude Girl*, sums up her life. In the slang of the Caribbean region, rude can mean strong and assertive. In a music world full of men, Ivy has had to be the original rude girl to gain respect and establish her place among the great stars of reggaeton. But the strength people see today is not only due to her role as the sole woman of reggaeton. The obstacles she faced in her early life also added to her confidence in both her personal life and in her music.

Puerto Rican Roots

Ivy Queen traces much of her current success back to her early years. Although her background did not give her a promising start, through determination, skill, luck, and hard work, Ivy Queen shot to fame—and she believes the obstacles she faced as a child and as a young woman are what have made her strong.

FROM THERE TO HERE

The reggaeton star was born on March 4, 1972, in Añasco, Puerto Rico. Her given name was Martha Ivelisse Pesante; she later used her middle name Ivelisse to create her stage name. As a little girl, she and her family moved to New York City, but they moved back to Añasco when she was a teenager, giving her ties to both the Spanish- and English-speaking worlds.

Her childhood was difficult and filled with poverty. During her teenage years, which were mostly spent back in Puerto Rico, Ivy had to quit going to school during the day and enroll

From her youngest days, Ivy Queen had the desire to express herself. For Ivy Queen, writing poetry was one way she dealt with her difficult life. Eventually the poems became songs.

in night school so that she could finish her education and take care of her five younger siblings at the same time. After her parents' divorce, she and her brothers and sisters became familiar with the pains of being hungry.

Ivy had known since she was small that she wanted to perform music, despite the obvious obstacles facing her. Somehow, in between taking care of a large family and finishing schoolwork, she found the time to explore music. When she told her mother she wanted to follow her dreams and become a musician, her mother supported her; her mother had confidence in her daughter's talent and ambition.

So Ivy wrote poetry and lyrics in high school, finding a way to express herself during her difficult adolescence that also prepared her for her later career as a musician. Even today, she continues to write many of her own songs, singing only about subjects that she feels are important, and letting her own emotions shine through to her audience.

Although her father left her mother, he had a hand in Ivy's early life as a musician. She often performed with him in places around the Añasco community, singing along with him as he played his guitar. Sometimes, she sang pieces she had written herself. The experience of playing in front of a hometown crowd slowly introduced her to performing her own music for bigger audiences.

Artists Who Influenced Ivy Queen

Some of Ivy Queen's strength as a woman is drawn from other Latina singers. She cites Selena, the famous *Tejano* singer who was shot and killed in 1995, as one of her inspirations. Besides being a proud woman who dared to be strong and independent, like Ivy and reggaeton, Selena was one of the first women to achieve success in the male-dominated Tejano genre. Selena was able to cross boundaries between cultures, something that Ivy is also trying to do. Although English was Selena's first language, she honored her heritage by producing her first albums in Spanish. She was one of the first musicians who managed to be successful both in the United States and in Latin America; she was in the process of creating an English album when she was killed. Ivy is intentionally following in Selena's footsteps. She even sang a **cover** of one of Selena's songs, "Si una Vez," on one of her albums. Ivy has said, "I've always identified with strong women. I admired Selena because she had that famous crossover success."

Celia Cruz is another strong woman who inspired Ivy. Cruz, born in Cuba in the 1920s, was one of the only female salsa singers, just as Ivy Queen is the only female reggaeton artist. Like Selena, Celia was also a cross-cultural hit, considered one of the most well-known Latina singers of all time. Ivy is doing her best to take Cruz's place!

Ivy also draws on other reggaeton musicians for strength and inspiration. As a teenager, when she watched Vico C, a well-known rap and reggaeton artist, perform on television, she told her father she wanted to do what she was seeing on TV: rhyme and sing for a bigger audience. She wanted to be like Vico C, singing her own style of music for her own generation. A few years later, she would perform with Vico C himself on her single "Somos Raperos Pero No Delincuentes," giving her the chance to fulfill her youthful dream.

Family Ties and Childhood

Ivy also finds strength in her family. She has said that her mother and the support she gave her were important parts of her success. Without the support of her family, she might not have had so much confidence in herself, nor would have been able to move out on her own from her hometown to San Juan.

IVY QUEEN

Adolescence can be difficult for anyone, but if you're growing up in poverty, like Ivy Queen did in a poor community in Puerto Rico similar to this one, the future can seem hopeless. She has proved that, if you work hard, things really can get better.

Even though her childhood was rough, it taught Ivy lessons she would take with her throughout her current career. She told the *Houston Chronicle* that she sings about

> "Not being able to get a job because you have tattoos or piercings. About growing up in a family where the parents are divorced, and having no money, not even for bread, like I did, and having to care for younger siblings."

The Beginning of a Career

Ivy Queen started small in Puerto Rico. At eighteen, she took a chance and left her home in Añasco. She moved to San Juan, Puerto Rico's capital, and began writing songs for other artists and competing in local talent shows. She eventually met DJ Negro, a rapper and music producer who realized she could go far with her singing. He introduced her to the owner of a popular local club called The Noise, where she started singing and was soon involved with the early reggaeton movement.

Ivy was featured on the fifth CD in a series focusing on artists from The Noise, a group of about twenty singers. As always, she was the only woman in the group. Her single on the CD, "Somos Raperos Pero No Delincuentes" ("We Are Rappers, Not Delinquents"), became a hit, foretelling her future rise to fame.

Ivy continued performing with The Noise for a few years, but eventually she became troubled by her association with the group. The artists in The Noise were known for their violent and sexual songs, so Ivy decided to split from the group and work toward a solo career with help from DJ Negro, the man who had first discovered her. In her later career, she continued to ignore the foul and **crude** language of some of her fellow artists, focusing instead on the message she wanted to communicate to her audience. This attitude earned her praise from many people who disliked songs with sexual lyrics.

First Big Break

Ivy Queen released her first solo album, *En mi imperio* (In My Empire), soon after splitting from The Noise. Even on this first album, Ivy showed she truly wanted her songs to reach out to people; she sang about social problems and women's issues, but did so in language that was not offensive. Her audience responded, and the album sold more than 100,000 copies.

In one short year, Ivy not only became famous, but she also won the title "People's Favorite Rapper," given to her by *Artista* magazine in 1997. Her career was looking up, and promised to keep growing.

On the Rise

Ivy didn't take much of a break before starting on her second album. After all, in music you're only as good as your latest album. She was dedicated to her work, not just to the fame that came with it. Two years after the first album debuted, she released *The Original Rude Girl*. The album featured a duet with Wyclef Jean, a well-known rap artist. Luck and skill worked together in her life, as they so often did, and this time this duet was the result.

It all started at a Wyclef Jean concert in Puerto Rico when audience members were invited on stage to try to keep up with Jean. Ivy's friends persuaded her to go up; she began to sing and dance, or "flow," as reggaeton terms it. Jean was so impressed he invited her to collaborate with him on a song. While that didn't happen immediately, he agreed to do the duet on Ivy's album after meeting her again when they both were featured in a concert at New York City's Madison Square Garden.

The duet with Jean spread Ivy's name beyond Puerto Rico. People in other Latin American countries, as well as in the

FROM THERE TO HERE   37

Luck has had a little something to do with Ivy Queen's career. One of her first big breaks came after she was one of the audience members who went onstage to perform with Wyclef Jean. The rap star was very impressed and promised to work with her.

United States, began to recognize her. In 2000, she moved back to New York City to collaborate with other artists living and working there. She released an album every few years, including *Sentimiento* (Emotion), which she put out in 2007. Each album stayed true to the style of reggaeton while containing unique lyrics from a female point of view. One album, *Flashback*, is a **compilation** of old favorites with new songs. *Flashback* shows perfectly how Ivy's career has developed. She is now a well-known star who has produced several hit songs, but who is still writing and singing new songs.

Beyond Music

Ivy's accomplishments stretch beyond her music. Her powerful messages have earned people's respect, and she is now recognized as one of the leading people in Latin America. *Latina* magazine chose her as one of the most important Latina women in today's world for her role in spreading awareness about women's issues. The Campaign to Fight Domestic Violence Against Women in Puerto Rico chose her to be its leader, giving Ivy the opportunity to put her words into action, and stand up for women's right to dignity, safety, and happiness.

The success of Ivy's albums has allowed her to spend more time pursuing other related interests as well. She is now in charge of a music production company, called Filtro Musik, where she has opportunities to work behind the scenes instead of in her usual role on stage. The company will give her a chance to start other stars on their own careers.

Gender Issues

Many of Ivy's songs are about women's issues: physical and emotional abuse, dependency on men, cheating. Clearly, her experiences as a woman inspired her to write powerful lyrics and sing them with emotion. Growing up in Puerto Rico and in the United States, she saw how women were treated—and she wanted to do something about it. She passionately includes feminist messages in her songs, hoping to inspire women to overcome oppression, to stand up for themselves, to shake free of dependency on the men around them.

Emotions

Perhaps the thing that has influenced Ivy Queen's music the most is Ivy Queen herself. She told *Billboard*,

> "I always have something to say, something to contribute. I never came with empty rhythm or lyrics. Men

One of the criticisms that hip-hop and reggaeton share is that many of their song lyrics seem to be demeaning to women. Ivy's songs deal with women, too, but they are songs of strength and empowerment.

Ivy Queen's songs strike a chord with her fans. She has a talent for creating songs that speak to the lives of those who follow her career. Her lyrics, along with her incredibly powerful voice, make it easy to understand why she has so many devoted fans.

saw that the girl could write and sing and go to the platform and kill, as we say."

Her emotions and passions sing out loud in every song. She has said, "I sing what's real, what I feel in the moment. My songs are a reflection of what happens day to day."

Ivy's fans also inspire her. She has said, "I have nothing but love for the fans. . . . They allow me to do what I do best and let me bring home my daily bread." While she is dedicated to her music for its own sake, she also understands the impact it has on her fans. She is more than willing to acknowledge how important they are to her; without her fans, her music would have no audience. They are the ones who have made Ivy and reggaeton so popular, and they are the ones who will help shape her career's future.

It hasn't happened over night, but Ivy Queen has seen her popularity rise all over the world. Award shows now have categories for reggaeton, and it's only a matter of time before Ivy Queen brings home her share of the statuettes.

The Future of Ivy Queen and Reggaeton

Ivy Queen—not to mention the entire world of reggaeton—is poised, ready to stake claim around the world. Every day, more and more people outside Latin America listen to reggaeton, giving it a promising future. In many ways, reggaeton's future will be Ivy's—and Ivy's will help shape reggaeton's.

Recent Struggles

Ivy Queen's difficulties didn't end with her childhood. Even though her career is now wildly successful and she has left behind the poverty and hunger of her earlier years, she has still had to face difficult personal challenges. Recently, her mother fought breast cancer, so Ivy had to juggle taking care of her mother and continuing her career, just as she had once balanced school and helping her family. Ivy also went through a divorce from her husband and producer Omar Navarro. The divorce, which was the subject of much media coverage, affected both her personal and professional lives.

These more recent obstacles, just like those of her earlier life, only helped make her stronger. In fact, she said that although her divorce was the hardest challenge she'd ever faced, she had learned to use her experiences to write new songs. In the end, her difficulties allow her to connect with more people who have gone through similar things in their life.

Personality

Throughout her career, Ivy has had a strong sense of responsibility and dedication to her career and her fans. Her executive producer said, "What I most admire about her is her sense of responsibility. . . . She has encountered many obstacles in life, and yet, she has always surmounted them gracefully." The sense of responsibility she learned as a teen taking care of her family has given her the strength to work hard in her career.

And she has worked *very* hard. She had to stick with reggaeton for more than a decade before it became popular. Only within the past few years has reggaeton begun to regularly show up on radios and in music stores, so in those early days, Ivy had to rely only on her passion for her music and her dedication to keep her motivated to continue.

Ivy seems to have a never-ending supply of energy, taking on many projects at once. She regularly tours to promote her latest albums, she **collaborates** with other artists, she appears on talk shows, and she attends award shows like the Latin Grammys. This makes for a demanding and exhausting travel schedule. For years, Ivy knew she had to work hard, find enough energy, to make a name for herself. Now that she's made that name, she has to make sure she keeps the

THE FUTURE OF IVY QUEEN AND REGGAETON

spot she earned in reggaeton, something she frequently says is made more difficult because she is a woman. She has said,

> "With this music thing, you can't just take it as a hobby and think you're going to make a bunch of money to buy some shoes or whatever. All your benefits come later, but for now, you have to work and sacrifice."

She often shares this message with her fans, hoping they will learn from her experiences.

Image

Although Ivy's dedication, hard work, and energy have been constants in her life, not everything about her has remained the same. As she has become older and grown as an individual, her image has changed. At the beginning of her career, she had a rough, street look, which helped her to fight her way to the top among so many men. She wore more masculine street clothes, and her fingernails were always several inches long. Today, she has traded that image for a *diva* look. She cut her nails and now tends to wear more feminine outfits. Part of her change in style can be credited to the fact that she's been growing up—but she also describes herself as someone who loves to simply experiment with her appearance, mixing up her look and surprising her fans. When someone asked her why she had changed her look, she said, "A woman's vanity. Don't expect to see me always the same because I am really crazy."

A Connection with Fans

Life in Puerto Rico, New York, and in the spotlight has shaped the person Ivy Queen has become. That person shines through to the audience when she performs. Besides her obvious dedication to her career, her music, and her message, Ivy is

IVY QUEEN

Few artists in any music genre have the connection with their fans that Ivy Queen has. In 2004 and 2005, her loyal fan base nominated her for People's Choice Reggaeton Awards.

THE FUTURE OF IVY QUEEN AND REGGAETON

committed to her fans. She connects well with them, earning her a loyal following among young people. The vice president of Univision Music Group, the company that currently distributes her albums, claimed she presents the same person on stage and off. He said, "She has this innate charisma that touches people in a way that you don't frequently see in other artists."

Her popularity with fans is what helps her sell albums and win awards. It was her fans who nominated her for People's Choice Reggaeton Awards in 2004 and 2005, proving their loyalty to her. The thousands of fans who show up to hear her at concerts also show how much support she has.

Ivy's fans, especially the female ones, readily identify with the star's poor background, the family issues with which she dealt, and her struggles to achieve an education and success in a male-dominated field. Many young women see her as an inspiration, someone who overcame the same things they may currently be facing.

Fans also relate to the topics of Ivy's songs, particularly the ones that describe the issues involved in romantic relationships. Ivy's parents raised her to love passionately, she says, and she wants her fans "to have songs that express what they are going through when they are in love." Although Ivy sings about love, her strength and independence shine through; it's clear that Ivy will never let herself be overshadowed by a man, no matter how much she loves him!

Ivy Queen's Future

Ivy Queen may no longer be a rebellious teenager, but she shows no signs of slowing down any time soon. Her energy and enthusiasm haven't begun to fade. Although she is in her thirties and has been a part of reggaeton since its earliest days, she continues to take the spotlight in an industry often dominated by younger artists. As of 2007, she had two more albums in the works, including *Drama Queen*, an album featuring duets with other female artists across many music genres.

Meanwhile, while still writing and performing her own music, Ivy is also planning on branching out beyond music, using her success to promote other things. She is working on a makeup line, called Queen, and a clothing line that reflects the type of clothes she normally wears. She says she wants to spread her image, not just her message, to the public, expanding the influence of reggaeton to fashion.

The Future of Reggaeton?

With the help of artists like Ivy Queen, reggaeton has spread beyond Puerto Rico and the Caribbean. People in Central, South, and North America are listening to it, as well as people from Europe, especially in Spain and Italy.

Some people, though, are predicting the decline of reggaeton. During 2005 and 2006, radios and clubs stopped playing reggaeton as often, and the genre didn't have any big hits. But reggaeton's artists remain positive. Ivy Queen has said she isn't worried; she believes all music goes through highs and lows. "There's no doubt there are people out there who listen to [reggaeton] and support it," she said.

The next few years will show whether this genre simply fades away, a passing fad that was popular for a few years—or whether it will continue to grow and become one of the next big global music movements. Its willingness to blend with other genres may dilute its unique character—but may also ultimately make reggaeton more resilient.

Cross-Genre

Because reggaeton has so many close musical cousins, like hip-hop and reggae, its artists can easily work with singers from other genres. Luny Tunes, for instance, a popular reggaeton duo, works with famous artists like Jennifer Lopez and Black Eyed Peas. **Remixes** of reggaeton songs in other genres are

THE FUTURE OF IVY QUEEN AND REGGAETON

now showing up in clubs. People are dancing to reggaeton remixes by Evanescence, Shakira, and Alicia Keys.

Reggaeton singers are also taking elements from other types of music and using them in their own songs. Music from the Caribbean region is particularly likely to show up. Recently, different styles of music, like **bachata** from the Dominican Republic and salsa, have been used in many reggaeton songs, and reggaeton tracks are influenced by everything from pop to techno.

Reggaeton has influenced the work of other performers whose names might not come to mind when thinking about the genre and its musicians. Jennifer Lopez is just one artist who has added some reggaeton kick to her music.

Artists from other genres are using reggaeton in their music as well. In Puerto Rico, reggaeton is so popular that more traditional salsa remixes of reggaeton songs are appearing on the island. In the United States, American artists are using reggaeton beats in their own songs; people like Britney Spears, Ricky Martin, and R. Kelly have hints of reggaeton rhythms in their songs, bringing reggaeton to a bigger audience. American artists are even collaborating with reggaeton artists on their own albums. Fat Joe, R. Kelly, and Nas have done collaborations, helping North American audiences become more familiar with reggaeton's rhythms.

In today's world, immigration has become a hotly debated topic. Waves of immigrants entering the United States from Latin America have forced Americans to think about what it means to have millions of new people move across the border into their country. The spread of reggaeton is related to this issue, since it, like immigrants, crosses the border from Latin America into the United States. Is it welcome there? Are Hispanic immigrants? North Americans aren't always certain of the answers to these questions, but whether they like it or not, Latinos—and their language, their food, their culture, and their music—are part of North America's future.

In 2006, Ivy Queen took part in a controversial project that added fire to the argument about Hispanic immigrants: a Spanish version of the national anthem called "Nuestro Himno" ("Our Hymn"). The song spread to radio stations throughout the United States; the sale of the CD containing "Nuestro Himno" and other songs about immigration were sold for ten dollars each, and a percentage of the money from the sales went to a foundation to help immigrants. And many Americans responded with outrage.

Some Americans felt that by taking the national anthem and putting it into a language other than the one in which it

THE FUTURE OF IVY QUEEN AND REGGAETON

was originally written, the producer, Ivy Queen, and the other artists who had participated had been disrespectful; some even said they had committed an act that was anti-American and unpatriotic. Others said that the Spanish version of the national anthem was an effort on the part of the artists to steal American culture; they said Ivy Queen and the others were trying to make American culture adapt to them, instead of trying to adapt to American culture. Even politicians got involved. Massachusetts senator Edward Kennedy called "Nuestro Himno" "un-American," and President Bush said the national anthem should only be in English (despite the fact that several U.S. government Web sites have versions of the national anthem not only in Spanish, but in languages ranging from Russian to Swahili).

Other people liked the anthem, though, and defended it. By translating the national anthem into Spanish, people argued, some immigrants to the United States would be able to understand the message of the national anthem for the first time. After all, said some Americans, isn't that the whole point of America: to welcome everyone, regardless of skin color, regardless of religion, regardless of language? Ultimately, don't we all share the same values—and isn't that what makes America strong? In the end, Ivy's voice served as a bridge between Hispanic American and Anglo Americans, helping to bring us all closer together.

Connections Between Cultures

Immigrants who grew up in places like Puerto Rico already know and love reggaeton, and so they bring the music with them when they move to the United States. They spread it to family members and friends on the mainland, which helps explain why reggaeton is especially popular in places like New York City, Miami, and the Southwest, where Latin Americans make up a large percentage of the populations.

Another reason why reggaeton has become popular in the United States is because of the growing population of young second-generation Latinos who were born in America. They usually speak both Spanish and English, and they understand American culture better than their parents—but they still feel ties to their Latin American roots and identify with other Latinos. Reggaeton provides the perfect link between their U.S. and Latin American identities. Most songs are sung in Spanish and are from countries like Puerto Rico, but they are also linked to American forms of music, such as hip-hop, and have more and more ties to American artists.

But immigrants aren't the only reason for reggaeton's rise in popularity. Young people in the United States who enjoy hip-hop are often attracted to reggaeton as well, particularly if they have heard their favorite artists singing with reggaeton artists. The same issues—social oppression, sex, and crime—inspire both styles. Computers, cell phones, and television have helped to spread reggaeton across the globe, making it easy for young people to discover and keep listening to artists like Ivy Queen.

The Language Debate

During the first half of 2005, shipments of Latin music increased dramatically. The popularity of reggaeton helped those shipments increase by 27.7 percent, meaning that more and more people in the United States are being exposed to music from Latin American countries. That usually means music sung in Spanish.

One of the biggest issues with immigration is whether or not immigrants should be expected to learn English and whether American citizens should learn Spanish. The fact that reggaeton, which is sung mostly in Spanish, is growing in popularity shows that many Americans don't mind the increasing influence of a different language, at least when it comes to the dance floor.

THE FUTURE OF IVY QUEEN AND REGGAETON

53

There's no denying the influence Latino culture has had in the United States. But when a group of Latino musicians, including Ivy Queen, recorded a Spanish version of the national anthem, some critics thought they had gone too far.

IVY QUEEN

DAILY NEWS

LATINO *LIFE*, NEW YORK *STYLE*
WWW.NYDAILYNEWS.COM • JUNE 2005

vny
VIVA NEW YORK

FREDDY FERRER:
Still in the Race?
by Juan González

IVY QUEEN
Even the Kings of Reggaetón Bow Down

Ivy Queen stands for what's good about reggaeton—what's good about music as a whole. Her music, and her life, inspire and empower people. And the world is taking notice—including New York City's *Daily News*.

The Rhythm of Harmony

Of course, reggaeton's main draw is its danceable beat. Many Americans who go to clubs that play reggaeton don't understand the lyrics they're hearing, but they like the music's rhythm and dancing to it is fun. And meanwhile, these English-speaking Americans are being exposed to Spanish; it's becoming a part of their world, so that it seems less "alien," more "normal." Reggaeton is bringing Spanish and English speakers together.

In the end, reggaeton is a voice for justice, the proud heartbeat of the Latino streets. Ivy Queen and other reggaeton musicians are using the rhythms of their music to bring people together, breaking language, cultural, and genre barriers. Ultimately, maybe it doesn't matter if reggaeton becomes a major world music style. After all, it has already inspired many young people around the globe.

CHRONOLOGY

March 4, 1972   Martha Ivelisse Pesante—Ivy Queen—is born in Puerto Rico.

late 1970s   Rap and hip-hop begin in the United States.

1980s   Reggaeton begins in Puerto Rico.

1995   Tejano artist Selena, a major influence on Ivy Queen, is murdered by her fan club president.

1997   Ivy Queen releases her first album.

Wins People's Favorite Rapper Award from *Artista* magazine.

2000   Ivy Queen moves back to the United States.

2004   Fans nominate Ivy Queen for People's Choice Reggaeton Awards; they do so again in 2005.

2006   Ivy Queen joins other Spanish-speaking artists to record a Spanish version of the U.S. National Anthem.

Nov. 3, 2006   The Latin Grammy Awards are held in New York City for the first time, with tickets available to the public.

ACCOMPLISHMENTS AND AWARDS

Albums

1997 *En Mi Imperio*
1998 *The Original Rude Girl*
2004 *Diva*
2004 *Real*
2005 *Flashback*
2005 *The Best of Ivy Queen*
2007 *Sentimiento*

DVD

2004 *Diva*

Awards and Recognition

1997 The National Festival of Rap and Reggae: Rap Singer of the Year; *Artista* magazine: Artista '97 Award for People's Favorite Rap Singer.

2006 Premios Juventud Awards: Diva Award.

Books

Castillo-Garstow, Melissa. "Latinos in Hip Hop to Reggaeton." *Latin Beat*, 2005.

Chang, Jeff. *Can't Stop Won't Stop: A History of the Hip-Hop Generation*. New York: Picador, 2005.

Kallen, Stuart A. *The History of Latin Music*. Farmington Hills, Mich.: Thomson Gale, 2006.

Kusek, Dave, and Gerd Leonhard. *The Future of Music: Manifesto for the Digital Music Revolution*. Boston, Mass.: Berkley Press, 2005.

Light, Alan (ed.). *The Vibe History of Hip Hop*. New York: Three Rivers Press, 1999.

FURTHER READING/INTERNET RESOURCES

Web Sites

Ivy Queen on MTV
www.mtv.com/music/artist/queen_ivy/artist.jhtml

Ivy Queen on MySpace
profile.myspace.com/index.cfm?fuseaction=user.viewprofile&friendID=29362533

Music of Puerto Rico—Ivy Queen
www.musicofpuertorico.com/index.php/artists/queen_ivy

Reggaeton History
www.tqnyc.org/NYC063107/reggaeton_history.htm

Reggaeton Online
www.reggaetonline.net

Glossary

bachata—A form of music and dance that originated in the countryside and rural neighborhoods of Dominican Republic.

collaborates—Works with others to create something.

compilation—Something created by gathering things from different places.

cover—A recording of a song that was previously recorded by someone else.

crude—Vulgar or obscene.

culture—The shared beliefs, customs, practices, and social behavior of a particular nation or people.

dancehall—A form of music that developed in Jamaica, similar to rap and faster than reggae.

diva—An extremely glamorous woman singer.

ethnicities—Groups based on shared cultural beliefs.

genre—One of the categories into which artistic works can be divided into on the basis of form, style, or subject matter.

graphically—Related with descriptive details, especially exciting or unpleasant ones.

GLOSSARY

mainstream—The ideas, actions, and values that are most widely accepted by a group or society.

medley—A continuous piece of music consisting of two or more different songs played one after the other.

norteño—A genre of Mexican music, featuring the accordion and the bajo sexto, that originated in the rural areas of Mexico.

oppression—The condition of being dominated by a person or group of people.

reggae—A form of music originating in Jamaica that combines elements of rock, calypso, and soul.

remixes—New versions of a piece of music that feature a change in the emphasis of the sound or adding new tracks.

salsa—A type of Latin American dance music that combines elements of jazz and rock with the rhythms of African-Cuban melodies.

Tejano—A style of Mexican American music with prominent accordion parts, influenced by polka, country and traditional Mexican music.

Index

Caribbean 13, 14, 15, 16, 30, 48, 49

Daddy Yankee 17, 18
Dem bow 16, 17
DJ Kool Herc 23
Drama Queen 47

En Mi Imperio 36

Flashback 38

hip-hop
   controversy 24–27
   history 23–24
   international 24
   versus reggaeton 23–27

Immigrants 50, 51, 52
Ivy Queen (Martha Pesante)
   early career 35–38
   early life 30–32
   future 47–48
   influences on 32–33
   personality 44–45
   recent struggles 43–44
   voice 30
   and women's issues 29–30, 38–39, 47

Jean, Wyclef 36, 37

Latin Grammy Awards 9, 10, 11, 12, 13, 44

Madison Square Garden 9, 19, 36

New York City 9, 10, 11, 12, 18, 19, 22, 23, 26, 31, 34, 36, 38, 40, 45, 46, 51
The Noise 35, 36
"Nuestro Himno" 50, 51

Original Rude Girl 30, 36

People's Choice Reggaeton Awards 46, 47
Puerto Rico 13, 14, 15, 16, 18, 19, 20, 22, 24, 27, 31, 34, 35, 36, 38, 45, 48, 50, 51, 52

reggae 16, 23, 48
reggaeton
   in America 17–19, 51–52
   characteristics 15–17, 19–20
   controversy 20–23
   future 48–50
   history 16–17
   versus hip-hop 23–27

INDEX

Salsa 13, 16, 20, 33, 49, 50
San Juan 33, 35
Selena 32, 33

Sentimiento 30, 38
"Somos Raperos Pero no Delincuentes" 33, 35

About the Author

Kim Etingoff lives in New York, where she is studying anthropology. She works in a library and has written many other books for young adults.

Picture Credits

Corbis: front cover, pp. 2, 8, 28, 40
Daily News: p. 54
iStockphoto: pp. 21, 46
    Diederich, Diane: p. 22
    Elefante, Vito: p. 26
    Estey, Juan: p. 53
    Feketa, Petro: p. 31
    Rodriguez, John: p. 34
    Schlax, Nick: p. 17
    Schmidt, Chris: p. 39
    Stein, Daniel: p. 12
    Zemdega, Andrejs: p. 25
    Zivana, Ufuk: p. 14
Jupiter Images: p. 40
Mayer, Janet / PR Photos: pp. 11, 18, 49
PR Photos: p. 37

To the best knowledge of the publisher, all other images are in the public domain. If any image has been inadvertently uncredited, please notify Harding House Publishing Service, Vestal, New York 13850, so that rectification can be made for future printings.